Images Of Life

Poems

By

LaVern Spencer McCarthy

Copyright 2017

By

LaVern Spencer McCarthy

All Rights Reserved

No part of this book may be reproduced by any means without written permission of the author.

ISBN 978-1-365-95806-9

The author may be contacted at:

lavernmccarthy33@hotmail.com

For Everyone Who Enjoys Poetry

Dedication

To Anthony Dickson
In Loving Memory
And
Rochelle Dickson,
His Shining Light

Table Of Contents

Life Scenes

Stars And Wishes 9
He Plays A Flute In Istanbul 10
An Old Man's Christmas Eve 11
Life's Special Treasures 12
Bereaved 13
A Poet Composes 14
Aging Musician 15
The Old Man Who Sleeps In My Shed 16
Aunt Mary's Mission 17
Storm Cellar—1948 18
Abel's Bones 19
Departed 20
A Different Path 21
Enraptured 22
Deceased 23
My Lost Love 24
The Answer 25
On Our 27th Wedding Anniversary 26
Some Starlit Night 27
This Rainy Night 28
A Promise 29
The Greatest Love 30
Blessings 31
Racing Home 32
Delbert Reads His National Geographic 33
He Died In The Cold, Bering Sea 34
Not Long From Now, A Garden 35
Remembered Love 36
I Watch Him Sleep 37
Remember Me 38

Reflections Of Nature

Nature's Poetry	41
Conversation	42
In Search Of April	43
November	44
Down The Rolling River	45
October Moments	46
Condemned	47
Green Mesquite	48
Coyote Songs	49
November Hills	50
Earth Songs	51
Gazing Upward	52
haiku—a fledgling sparrow	53
haiku—snow covered aspen	53
The Frogs' Farewell	54
Night Storm	55
Creating Spring	56
Ants In The Sugar Bowl	57
The Sea's Elusive Treasures	58
Nature's Melodies	59
Whispering Leaves	60
A Summer Tale	61
The Style Of May	62
The Joy Of Bluebonnets	63
The Locust	64
Spring's Arrival	65
Winter Sunset	66
A Warty Frog Explains Why It Needs A Kiss	67
Nature's Tantrum	68

Animal Portrayals

Night Creatures 71
A Fowl Situation 72
Lament Of An Old, Lost Dog 73
Curly 74
Old Jake 75
Siesta In The Garden 76
The Vulture 77
Billy's Revenge 78
Heavenly Horses 79
To A Pushy Cat 80
Hippo Choir 81
The Abandoned Kittens 82
Why The Charmed Snake Does Not Escape 83
A Black Cat 84
My Feathered Helpers—Where Did They Go? ... 85
Missing 86
The Halloween Cat 87
Horned Toad Hangout 88
Mockingbird 89
A Rat's Reprieve 90
haiku—guarding its nestlings 91
She Won't Turn Loose Till It Thunders 92
Cicadas Say 93
haiku—pine trees waft perfume 94
Canine Intellectual 94
Ladybug 95
Song Of Summer 96
At The Picnic 97
Bird Of Prey 98
Robin 99

Views

The Psychedelic Party 103
Age, The Cat 104
Barbie 105
Little Boy Love—For Tony 106
Death Of A Vacuum Cleaner 107
In This Land 108
The Missing Poet 109
To Keep My Leaping Sheep 110
At Daybreak 111
The Ticking Of The Clock 112
Behold The Raging River 113
The Winner 114
Completing My Unfinished Poems 115
The New Year's Kiss 116
When Love Dies 117
Listening To The Police Band Radio 118
Toward Our Destinies 119
Dance, Gypsy 120
At Parting 121
October Memories 122
Competitive Brawl 123
Grandpa's Outfit 124
Shadows 125
Exhibition 126
Immortal Love 127
Day Dreams 128
In My Hammock 129
The Charms Of Spring 130
His Presence, Everywhere 131
At Twilight 132
In Tribute 133
Greener Grass 134
About the Author 135
Publishing History 136

the
Life Scenes

Stars And Wishes

Upon a ridge just north of town,
after the evening sun went down,
I saw a shooting star—it sped
south of Orion's sparkled head,
became a blaze in form most odd
like a white breath exhaled from God.
I made a wish for wondrous things—

fine mansions, yachts and diamond rings.
My wish came true. Riches untold,
ingots of silver, kegs of gold
were given me. The world was mine.
Thus, I proclaimed myself divine.
But, as I lived in vanity,
these treasures failed to comfort me.

Not one could ever take the place
of laughter on a loved one's face,
or cheer me when my nights were sad.
In spite of all the wealth I had,
greed's degradation took its toll,
making a pauper of my soul.
I often wander north of town

after the evening sun goes down.
I gaze at heaven shining fair
with countless wishes waiting there.
There comes a blaze in form most odd
like a white breath exhaled from God,
but wiser than before am I,
who watch the shooting stars go by.

He Plays A Flute In Istanbul

A small boy plays his flute and often weeps
because of war and what it took away.
His life is hard, and hunger never sleeps.

He sits upon the walk and barely reaps
enough to make his music making pay.
A small boy plays his flute and often weeps.

He thinks of those at home as evening creeps
along the streets where he must often stay.
His life is hard, and hunger never sleeps.

When someone takes his flute, his fury leaps
in all directions, followed by dismay.
A small boy plays his flute and often weeps.

He now must find another flute from heaps
of gadgets merchants tout in full display.
His life is hard, and hunger never sleeps.

His crown shall earn a star because he keeps
his family alive for one more day.
A small boy plays his flute and often weeps.
His life is hard, and hunger never sleeps.

An Old Man's Christmas Eve

He lives alone inside a rusty shack
with nothing but a puppy for a friend.
But, on this Christmas Eve the ghosts are back—
his family on whom his dreams depend.
Noel, with merriment like none before,
brings joy to him. As precious moments wane,
he does not seem to mind the north wind's roar,
or how death watches through the window pane.
Tonight is made for laughter, not for tears.
As everyone draws near, the past, defied
by loving memories of treasured years,
displayed upon a table side by side,

the portraits will not let his sorrow stay,
but warm him with the smiles of yesterday.

Life's Special Treasures

I do not need a keg of gold,
or diamonds in a velvet case.
I only crave a mockingbird
that leads me to a peaceful place
along the reaches of my soul
no thief can steal, or time, erase.

I do not care for grand estates
with riches flaunted everywhere.
They cannot hold me when I weep,
or soothe me with a Sunday prayer.
A hovel by the road will do
if God and all my friends are there.

I do not yearn for diadems
except for dew the meadow brings—
the sunlight and the morning star—
the harvest moon when autumn sings.
With all these treasures I am blessed
for life is full of special things.

Bereaved

He left her a widow
and she became his tombstone.
Cold, hard and proud,
she stoically weathers life,
always following him.
She speaks his name in
crumbled granite.
His epitaph is on her face.

A Poet Composes

Food crystallizes on the stove while she,
in search of perfect verse is soaring near
bright muses of a far off galaxy.
She pens blue stars to paper. No one here
dares interrupt her trance. The phone may ring.
She will not answer from the vast unknown.
Dust bunnies wait. The house needs vacuuming.
She fails to notice, when a higher zone
compels her mind to create. She must cope
with mystic visions heaven furnished her.
But, as her poem is finished, let us hope
she has forgotten realms of Jupiter,

for who can tend a house and bake the grain
with comet songs still whirling through the brain?

Aging Musician

He does not like the nursing home.
He cannot roam
for needed things,
but his heart sings
when kinfolk bring his violin.
He smiles and then
proceeds to play
his cares away,
performs for others, does not grieve.
The furrows leave
his aging brow.
He's happy now.

The Old Man Who Sleeps In My Shed

On winter nights he creeps about
my yard, and when the moon is out,
I watch him steal into the shed
where he has made a cozy bed
beside the rusted pipes and grout.

He has a place where walls are stout
away from streets where gangsters rout
the homeless to a darker dread
on winter nights.

On snowy ground, with cautious tread,
I leave for him a loaf of bread.
Though friends despair and neighbors flout
the situation, there's no doubt
by caring ways his soul is fed
on winter nights.

Aunt Mary's Mission

Aunt Mary always placed her cakes and pies
for cooling, on the kitchen window sill.
Somehow it came to her as no surprise
that hobos loved her treats and ate their fill.
They paid with posies, or a sparkled stone
put carefully beside an empty plate.
Those homeless men who rode the rails alone
were blessed by one who cared about their fate.
Aunt Mary kept a Bible by her side.
She prayed for those who crept around her door.
Her friends and relatives would often chide
regarding her endeavors for the poor,

but she would merely smile at us and say,
"I fed a hungry child of God today."

Storm Cellar—1948

When night storms brought
danger, Grandma forced us
into the 'fraidy hole.'

Down there scorpions ruled.
Centipedes crawled
down collars.
Dank things squiggled
across our arms.

Forgetting the beast outside,
we huddled around
our lantern like cavemen
at the dawn of creation,
afraid to move.

Later, when the storm had
passed, I went to sleep
and dreamed of clouds
with stinging tails.

Abel's Bones

Today we buried Abel
on a far, north hill
where he tended sheep
and spoke with God.
From my womb to the ground,
his bones cry for vengeance
while Cain wanders, untouchable
even unto death.

We pleaded, "God, have mercy.
Let us bury Abel by the river
that flows out of Eden
where we spent our innocent, glory days."
God did not answer
and the gates were closed.

Two sons were lost because of
what deceit led me to.
My soul drifts like chaff
on a bright, windy day.
As, sitting on a stone I weep,
from deep in the grass
the Serpent laughs.

Forgotten

I'd thought I was a memory,
a jewel my friends could own—
a glimmer in their velvet minds
now that my life is gone.

I'd thought they'd always speak of me
that I might dwell among
them daily in a spirit's way,
my name on every tongue.

But all they do is rattle on
about the things they've done
and how the grass upon the hill
grows yellow in the sun.

A Different Path

From youth, we walked together hand in hand
with souls entwined, as roses are in spring.
He took me to a far, enchanted land
sun swept with joy that only love could bring.

We danced across the world without a care,
our happiness assured forevermore,
for we had lives to live and dreams to share.
Then came a rougher road unseen before.

Why did I never hear the voice of fate?
I should have listened when the wind was high
above the mountain's misted crest. Of late,
on dreary nights I weep and wonder why

he lies asleep beneath a mossy stone
while I am left to find my way, alone.

Enraptured

The clouds are pink and blue wherein I lie
as close to heaven as a soul can be.
A shining angel sings a lullaby.

I drift across the reaches of the sky,
unmindful of earth's voices calling me.
The clouds are pink and blue wherein I lie.

I never knew that joy could reach this high,
but gladly welcome its exotic spree.
A shining angel sings a lullaby.

She fluffs my pillow with the south wind's sigh,
unveils a dream that only I can see.
The clouds are pink and blue wherein I lie.

I must go home again. I know that I
am still a mortal, bound by love's decree.
A shining angel sings a lullaby.

My son and daughter, birthed one hour, cry.
Our lives commingle for eternity.
The clouds are pink and blue wherein I lie.
A shining angel sings a lullaby.

Deceased

The workers at the seniors' home
are busy carting out
her memories. Indifferently
they toss old clothes about,
remove all photos from the shelves,
bag every shoe in sight,
remake the bed and spank the dust,
then pull the curtains tight.

Her days of pain are over now.
Her final hope has flown,
her treasures, flung into the void.
The past is dead and gone.
The workers laugh and leave the room.
Nobody thinks to pray.
How easily they tidied up
and put her life away.

My Lost Love

On lonely nights my love returns to me
out of the misty realms of yesterday.
I hold him once again in memory.

We dance among the stars. A melody
drifts down from space where shining angels play.
On lonely nights my love returns to me.

Our passionate embraces set us free
to whisper of the years that could not stay.
I hold him once again in memory.

We shed no tears for what will never be,
but laugh until the dawn is pearly gray.
On lonely nights my love returns to me.

We trek the bright hills of eternity
to find what scenes of joy they might convey.
I hold him once again in memory.

Only in dreams' disclosures do I see
the one who stole my heart and ran away.
On lonely nights my love returns to me.
I hold him once again in memory.

The Answer

When I was very young, I thought that I
was meant to own a mansion by the bay,
or be an astronaut who blazed the sky,
renowned for finding kingdoms far away.

The fates had other plans. My lot has been
a shack beside the road. My only flight,
a futile dream that stretched its wings within
my soul, then swiftly vanished into night.

I waited long for revelation's sign,
misunderstood the force compelling me,
but now I see. The answer grows divine.
At last, I know it is my destiny

to be a friend to others while I can
and live, according to the Master's plan.

On Our 27th Wedding Anniversary

Today was beautiful, my love.
The clouds above
were pure and white,
a true delight.
I bought red roses just for you
because I knew
of all the rest
you liked them best.
I put them on your grave and cried.
Although you died,
I love you still.
I always will.

Some Starlit Night

I hear a lonely melody
across the long years springing.
A bygone, lovely melody
straight to my heart is winging
of how, when daily chores were done,
we'd gather on the porch for fun
and after-supper singing.

Too many years have come and gone,
and yet my mind keeps bringing
my loved ones back from life's lost days.
I hear their voices ringing.
"Amazing Grace, I'll Fly Away,"
were fitting songs we'd often say
for after-supper singing.

I know they're all in heaven now.
My tear-filled eyes are stinging.
I hear the banjo Grandpa plays.
It sets the spheres to swinging.
My longing soul has just one prayer.
Some starlit night I'll meet him there
for after-supper singing.

This Rainy Night

The trucks along the highway make me weep.
Their wheels sing lonely melodies tonight.
I listen to the rain and cannot sleep.
Someone is lost who gave my world its light.

I wonder if his heart is still aglow
with foolish dreams that only dissipate.
I miss him, but I had to let him go.
I should have known regret would be my fate.

Each time I try to douse an inner fire,
it will not die. The embers linger still.
I search through haunted lands of old desire,
perceive his shadow drifting on the hill.

Perhaps he travels down love's road somewhere,
but I, who mourn, will never find him there.

A Promise

My mother had no green thumb to bestow
seed packet miracles. We only found
our souls in floral wild across the ground
of byways where our hearts said we must go.
She spoke of mystic blossoms, very fine.
If I would follow truth and seek the light,
of faith and love, then pray with all my might,
red roses of the spirit could be mine,
to bring me joy where only sorrow grew.
I thought her promise erred one summer day
before she blessed my life and passed away,
but now that I have found her meaning true,

I tend the garden she described to me—
exotic blooms of immortality.

The Greatest Love

We married on a summer day.
We vowed to never say goodbye.
I love him more than I can say.
We married on a summer day.
With souls entwined along the way,
we journey onward to the sky.
We married on a summer day.
We vowed to never say goodbye.

Blessings

I do not own a grand estate
with golden knobs at every door,
nor host of crystal chandeliers
that sparkle on a polished floor.
My furnishings are bleak and bare.
My humble home is dark and poor.

But I have rainbows in the mist—
a love song and a morning prayer—
a robin in the willow tree—
my darling's kisses, always there.
With all these things I know that I
could build a castle anywhere.

Racing Home

In summer when I was a boy,
with Brother by my side,
we'd race across the cotton fields,
or ramble far and wide
to gaze on sights the Good Lord made
that left us wonder eyed.

A campfire by the river's edge—
a fortress in a tree—
a log that made a pirate ship
upon a stormy sea—
those were the things that brought us joy
when we were young and free.

We had adventures by the score,
for that was childhood's way.
We laughed and dreamed of frogs and kings,
but we could only stay
until we heard the dinner bell
that called us home from play.

It carried faintly on the wind.
Its message was sincere—
of nurture and a caring heart.
With thoughts of love and cheer,
we raced along the forest trail
to someone we found dear.

We did not stop for labored breath,
or stubbing of a toe.
We might have had our boyish flaws,
but we were never slow
when Mama rang the dinner bell
in days of long ago.

Delbert Reads His National Geographic

Delbert is reading again, as he always does
at night when it rains. His candle sizzles his tears
as he weeps for wild elephants killed in Africa.
In Article 51 he sees dinosaur bones, tries
to reconstruct them, tries to breathe them alive.

Pages riffle in wind drifting through a window.
Delbert does not notice, but cocks an ear
for the whiz of a pygmy's dart, listens
     for the sound of time moving.

Rain stops. The sky wears a bright button moon.
Delbert sees nothing. His eyes are full of smoke.
Dazed, struck dumb by the scent of pine trees,
he stands barefoot. The spaces between his toes
are filled with yellow cowslips as he waits for
     Gypsies at the edge of the forest.

He Died In The Cold, Bering Sea

My mother sets a place for him tonight,
perhaps for consolation as we dine.
I watch until his plate has sunk from sight.
His napkin drifts, and sharks are in the wine.
The silver, laid with loves precision, rings
an S.O.S. against his saucer's rim.
His Dresden cup becomes a shroud that brings
a wave of grief as I remember him,
my brother, lost forever in the deep.
At last, the moments pass, and with a sigh
I clear the ship-wrecked table. As I weep,
from far away I hear his dreadful cry.

He swims in fear and cannot reach the shore,
succumbs to darkness, then is heard no more.

Not Long From Now, A Garden

There's no one in the garden shed.
I checked a while ago.
A battered rake is on the floor
beside a rusted hoe.
A coffee can holds trowels and tools
that help a garden grow.

An old, blue shirt is on the shelf.
It has a rip, or two.
A hat is clinging to a nail.
Its band is sweated through.
It seems the implements of toil
are rarely clean and new.

There's no one in the garden shed,
but spring is coming soon.
The man who walks among the rows
will whistle up a tune,
consult his almanac and plant
to phases of the moon.

He'll wear the shirt that needs a stitch.
The hat, he will extol
for shading him from summer's rays
as he pursues his goal—
a host of green and growing things
that satisfies the soul.

Remembered Love

He is not lost. I see him when I sleep.
In solitude and hope he beckons me.
I rush to him, emotions running deep.
O time, you have not dimmed his memory
nor altered any closeness of the past
that we fulfilled with true devotion's glow.
How foolish to believe love would not last.
The thrill is still the same as long ago.
I find in deepest moments of the night
there is no need to grieve that he is gone.
I will be happy in the morning light.
My fate is not to face this world alone,

for, when I yield unto a dream's command,
I reach across the years and touch his hand.

I Watch Him Sleep

Tonight while he sleeps
I watch his face
through moon's tender beams.
I wish I could suffuse him
with my life, my strength,
renew his ebbing spark
into a brand new star.

I fear his death. That great
terror shivers my bones.
He reaches for me, pulls me
back from a black abyss.
We snuggle soul to soul.
I soak up courage for dawn
when he awakens, to fight
      for another day.

Remember Me

When I have gone beyond the day
to brighter lands somewhere, I pray
remember me in some small way,

perhaps with laughter or a cry
of sorrow when the wind is high.
Recall me with a simple sigh.

The remnants of a song will do
to show how much I meant to you
when life was good and dreams came true.

Though I am bound by death's decree,
your smile will set my spirit free.
When I am gone, remember me.

Reflections Of Nature

Nature's Poetry

A sonnet has appeared upon the sky,
created in a way I did not see,
that I might read its lavender and try
to guess the end the sun composed for me.
The river chortles in iambic song.
The lyrics of the mystic meadow thrill.
Wild flowers captivate the whole day long
with villanelles of yellow on the hill.
All earth is poetry that shall endure.
The mountains rhyme with odes the valleys made,
awakening my Muse, but I am sure
these humble words I write will only fade

while nature scribes with an almighty pen
immortal verse that tells where God has been.

Conversation

A conversation has begun
where woods comprise a scene.
The leaves are talking to the wind
in syllables of green.

The gossip flows from twig to twig,
and by the garden wall
I hear the burly oak relate
the wildest tale of all.

Why should I listen to the field
for what the grass might say
when leafy tongues already tell
the story of the day?

In Search Of April

I have grown tired of winter's sullen gray,
those howling winds that never seem to care.
I need a touch of April in my day.

A robin, rapt in cheerful roundelay,
would lift my sodden spirit from despair.
I have grown tired of winter's sullen gray.

A fickle sun appears, but does not stay.
There lies a threat of snow upon the air.
I need a touch of April in my day.

I long for meadow flowers in a spray,
an antidote to season's frosty snare.
I have grown tired of winter's sullen gray.

Give me a morning bright with joy, I pray,
with busy springtime racing here and there.
I need a touch of April in my day,

or else I think that I shall run away
to continents less glacial and bare.
I have grown tired of winter's sullen gray.
I need a touch of April in my day.

November

November is a lady
unsure of what to wear.
Forever changing colors,
she strips her closets bare
until dead leaves are hanging
in states of disrepair.

She flings her gowns of crimson,
her shawls of autumn hues,
across the distant woodlands
in multicolored views
then dances on the meadow
in silver spangled shoes.

Down The Rolling River

A river beckons, but I cannot go.
Although I traveled down it once before,
my raft, upon the raging water's flow,
I promised I would linger on the shore.

Although I traveled down it once before,
ignoring dangers lurking everywhere,
I promised I would linger on the shore.
A river calls. I am forbidden there.

Ignoring dangers lurking everywhere,
I laughed my way toward the silver sea.
A river calls. I am forbidden there.
The rapids made a total fool of me.

I laughed my way toward the silver sea
until a boulder jarred me through and through.
The rapids made a total fool of me.
I clung upon the edge a day or two.

Until a boulder jarred me through and through,
I thought the river spirits wished me well.
I clung upon the edge a day or two,
sun-burned, delirious, and then I fell.

I thought the river spirits wished me well.
Those spirits either slept, or lazed about.
Sun-burned, delirious and then I fell.
A countryman appeared and fished me out.

Those spirits either slept or lazed about
my raft upon the raging water's flow.
A countryman appeared and fished me out.
A river beckons, but I cannot go.

October Moments

When the moon is school bus yellow,
sleepy children say their prayers,
waiting for October spirits
to arise from haunted lairs.

House cats dream of brooms and witches,
bare their claws and scratch the night.
Dead leaves skitter down dark alleys,
tiny ghouls in endless flight.

Old dogs hang around back porches,
shake and tremble, full of woe,
seeking solace from their masters,
every howl portending snow.

North wind whoops it up, carousing,
states a round of future goals,
murmurs at the eaves, conniving
mischief on unwary souls.

Hazy stars wink out their candles
while the silent hoot owl stares.
When the moon is school bus yellow,
sleepy children say their prayers.

Condemned

A killer bee
in black and yellow convict suit
languishes behind silvery bars
while warden spider denies parole.

Green Mesquite

Old timers love to sit and talk
about that native tree,
how, as it greens, the elements
begin a sudden spree.
Tornado alley opens wide
and sets the demons free.

The sky becomes an olio.
The river sings a song.
The grass is waiting on the hill,
will soon become a throng.
The earth is poised for season's change
when April comes along.

But, though the days are growing warm
with robins all a-tweet
while tulips raise their noble heads
and iris blooms are sweet,
it isn't really spring until
we see the green mesquite.

Coyote Songs

Coyotes sing of stormy spring,
tornadoes on the ground,
of wind and rain and flowing grain
when summer rolls around.

Coyotes moan of days now gone
in Texas of the past
where settlers' toil on fertile soil
ensured a dream would last.

Coyotes wail a lovely tale
that gives my heart a thrill—
with days replete with green mesquite,
bluebonnets on the hill.

Coyotes cry a lullaby.
In every eerie tune,
as I recall, they tell it all
while howling at the moon.

November Hills

My lonely trek there was not for thrills,
or late wild blooms for a rose bouquet.
I only went to admire those hills
of cedar green and November gray.

I did not go to remain or die,
but to gaze upon the great stone view,
and to watch the blackbirds swirl and fly
like a worn out cape with sky let through.

I did not go there to weep for spring
although I found traces of a tear
dried by the power of north wind's sting
bearing the first snowflake of the year.

My purpose was to fulfill a prayer
while storing the scene in memory,
and now that I left my footprints there,
I know the hills will remember me.

Earth Songs

I need a summer melody
to bring enchantment to my day.
No man-made music—not for me.
I need a summer melody,
a locust humming in a tree,
a skylark singing on its way.
I need a summer melody
to bring enchantment to my day.

Gazing Upward

What worlds are there beyond familiar sky?
Untraveled wonders wait for those who dare.
I would explore the countless stars if I
could only find a trail to take me there,
but merely to the mighty edge of space
that rims the universe. My aim would be
perhaps, to see the shadow of God's face
before He barred me from eternity,
or sit upon Uranus for a day
to hear an angel sing of love and light.
But, though I yearn for kingdoms far away
with upward reaching dreams that blaze the night

and pray for comet wings to help me soar,
this world will hold me here forever more.

2 haiku

a fledgling sparrow
sees its face in a rain pool
and pecks the water

snow covered aspen
ravens rest on every limb
black leaves of winter

The Frogs' Farewell

The bullfrogs croak in fear tonight,
forecasting winter's coming white,
prepare to burrow out of sight.

Along the creek where reeds are high
a cold, north wind begins to sigh,
evokes more tremors of goodbye.

That ceaseless dirge of what will be
conjures an icy memory,
a constant thought consuming me.

Before old winter shows its face
and drives me to my cozy place,
I, too, shall fear its wild embrace.

Night Storm

Beyond the distant mountain crest
a witch grows angry in the west.
She mutters from her thunder bed
then stirs, to fill the world with dread.

She grumbles loudly through the sky,
her rage aroused, her temper high.
She stomps around awhile and stews
in her best pair of lightning shoes,

ignites the night with fiery face
and shoves the clouds from place to place.
The wind runs howling none too soon
to tell the stars to hide the moon.

On, on she goes with bold desire
to set the universe on fire.
At last she tires and settles down
to sleep in her old ragged gown.

Her anger flickers as she sighs.
Beyond the hills her malice dies.
She, who has caused uncounted tears,
chuckles softly and disappears.

Creating Spring

Although November days have now decreed
the death of many things that I adore,
a hundred pretty words are all I need
to paint a garden for the world, and more.
A mighty brace of nouns will help construe
a scenic river running wild and free.
Then, I will build a lovely realm of dew
that sparkles from the mountains to the sea.
When winter wind is howling in despair,
an adjective or two will help it grow
into an April song of balmy air
that melts away the sorrow and the snow.

Then, on a sunny morning, I might make
a four-leaf clover for my spirit's sake.

Ants In The Sugar Bowl

Miles of black ants have come
to steal from my porcelain sugar bowl.
Each grabs a grain, scurries away
into unknown realms.

No doubt they thieve for their queen.
When she sees those sweet diamonds,
I'll bet she rolls in them, stuffs
herself, sports them as sparkly
bracelets on each antennae, emits
ant cackles of pure delight.

She is unaware that I could exterminate
her minions in seconds. But I only
watch the mindless toil, meditate
on creation's grand scheme.
Who am I to deny them their purpose?

The Sea's Elusive Treasures

I yearn for endless wealth, but I was told
that Neptune covets riches of the sea.
He bribes the octopi with grains of gold
to help him guard it for prosperity.
Yet, often in an altruistic mood,
the sea will fling her treasures to the shore
that those who search for miles in solitude
may find the things their hearts and minds adore.
I also stroll across the tawny sand
in search of sites where hidden treasures are.
I long to hold a diamond in my hand
with sparkles that were stolen from a star.

But none remain. The troves I seek are gone.
A bauble made of glass is all I own.

Nature's Melodies

The housefly tunes its buzz down low
because it knows that it must go.
I hear the cricket all night long
chirping its 'what happened?' song.
The field mouse squeaks on barren shelf
a loud operetta to itself,
and every time the wind blows through
it sings a dirge in bitter blue.
I think the sounds I often hear
are not discordant to the ear,
but, played in many different keys,
are nature's finest melodies.

Whispering Leaves

The leaves have cryptic messages
that few can understand,
but nature writes them anyway.
With sure and careful hand,
she places them in early spring
on trees across the land.

On summer nights when stars are out,
with many soughs and sighs,
the leaves will sing upon the wind
a song of paradise,
or whisper what the future holds,
for they are very wise.

Then, in the autumn of the year
when earth is growing cold,
if one will listen to the leaves,
true stories may be told—
the secrets of the universe
revealed in red and gold.

A Summer Tale

A paragraph of birds before the storm
foretells its fury to a startled world.
Above the mountains, cloud novellas form
with thunder syllables and lightning hurled
as markers, that explorers later on
might read a message cinders left behind.
Then falls the rain. With all pretensions gone,
the wind inscribes its will on humankind.
A final chapter passes through the hills,
caresses drooping flowers. From on high,
as peace descends, a welcome sun reveals
an epic rainbow printed on the sky.

The tale is told; the book has blown away.
Thus, ends the saga of a summer day.

The Style Of May

March's garb is scant and cold.
She shivers by the stair.
April's dress is green and blue
with crocus yellow flare.
May arrives in pansy pink
with clover in her hair.

The Joy Of Bluebonnets

Bluebonnets are the tears the angels cry
when rainbows they are climbing disappear.
Their blossoms are the color of the sky,
a sacrament to all who hold them dear.
They drift across the meadows far away,
but I have found them by my garden wall.
Though other sights might bless an April day,
their perfect beauty pleases most of all.
A vagabond at heart, I often stroll
through verdant fields on sunny days of spring.
Bluebonnets are a balm unto my soul.
When I behold their purity, I sing,

extol the angels with a sweet refrain
to let them know they have not wept in vain.

The Locust

The locust sings the whole daylong
and fills the summer hours with song.
He never sleeps—I thought he might—
but hangs upon a twig at night.
His greatest powers are then unfurled.
He serenades a sleeping world.

The house cat creeps on padded paws
to catch the locust in his jaws,
but Pouncing Tom will only find
a quivering shadow left behind.
The locust sings a wild refrain
when all the earth is parched for rain.

He sits upon a twig and wails
for thunder bolts and lightning trails.
The locust knows that he must go
when autumn comes with winds of snow.
He clings onto a barren tree
and makes a mourner out of me.

Spring's Arrival

That vixen, Spring, is on her way.
She sent a note of daffodils—
a paragraph of birds that say,
"That vixen, Spring, is on her way!"
This time I think she means to stay.
She banished winter from the hills.
That vixen, Spring, is on her way.
She sent a note of daffodils.

Winter Sunset

The sunset is electric gold,
a scene that none can duplicate.
As angels gain the western fold,
the sunset is electric gold.
It only means that God is bold
with hints of heaven's holy state.
The sunset is electric gold,
a scene that none can duplicate.

A Warty Frog Explains Why It Needs A Kiss

"I'll be a smooth-faced prince
if I am soundly kissed.
Then I won't need to see
my dermatologist."

Nature's Tantrum

The trees in the lane
are making it plain
that nature has thrown
a tantrum again.

She cowered the trees
with December breeze.
She hindered the pond
by making it freeze.

Why doesn't she try
to soften the sky?
I ponder the gray.
I stifle a sigh.

I'll watch with a will
each drab, withered hill,
each dried patch of grass,
each byway until

remorseful, she clears
her wrath and appears
to sprinkle the world
with life-giving tears.

Animal Portrayals

Night Creatures

Sometimes on winter nights
when coyotes run through
the grain fields, point
their devil snouts at the moon
and howl, I am consumed
by utter desolation.

A Fowl Situation

My hens were fertile in a former day.
With self-important airs that all can see,
they strut around the barn and do not lay.

I search for hidden nests in mounds of hay,
but hen-o-pause has set my chickens free.
My hens were fertile in a former day.

I often dream of omelets and pray
my birds resume their reproductive spree.
They strut around the barn and do not lay.

I ate their produce in a callous way.
Perhaps they grieve for chicks that could not be.
My hens were fertile in a former day.

Should I atone for what I did and pay
in tearful restitution, diner's fee?
They strut around the barn and do not lay.

They cast reproachful eyes at me. I say,
"A pot of biddy stew is fine with me!"
My hens were fertile in a former day.
They strut around the barn and do not lay.

Lament Of An Old, Lost Dog

The night is cold, and I am here alone.
I'm lost—I miss my home and family.
Starvation nears; my life is almost gone.
Won't someone please be kind and rescue me?

I'm lost—I miss my home and family.
A caring boy was always by my side.
Won't someone please be kind and rescue me?
The streets are cruel. Today I almost died.

A caring boy was always by my side.
I miss his laughter more than I can say.
The streets are cruel. Today I almost died.
A car came at me, but I ran away.

I miss his laughter more than I can say.
That special boy I knew—where did he go?
A car came at me, but I ran away.
My eyes are growing dim and I am slow.

That special boy I knew—where did he go?
I search for him, but he is never there.
My eyes are growing dim and I am slow.
I only hope someday someone will care.

I search for him, but he is never there.
Starvation nears; my life is almost gone.
I only hope someday someone will care.
The night is cold, and I am here alone.

Curly

A happy, young robin named Curly
went searching for worms bright and early.
He nibbled a live wire,
set his feathers on fire.
He now rises late and is surly.

Old Jake

The old, hound dog I loved is now asleep.
I buried him beneath a willow tree.
I often stand beside his grave and weep.

He bounds beside me when the nights are deep
along my forest floor of memory.
The old, hound dog I loved is now asleep.

His name was Jake. I hope the angels keep
him safe among the stars where he must be.
I often stand beside his grave and weep.

I miss him most when evening shadows creep
around the moon upon its dusky sea.
The old, hound dog I loved is now asleep.

The hills I climb without him are too steep.
The valleys sing of sorrow's melody.
I often stand beside his grave and weep.

Someday in paradise my Jake will leap
those alabaster gates and welcome me.
The old, hound dog I loved is now asleep.
I often stand beside his grave and weep.

Siesta In The Garden

A mother cat is dozing in the sun.
Her kittens tumble near her, having fun.
They chase her tail that slaps the garden wall,
then wrestle on and on, as kittens will.
Her eyes are closed. She does not mind at all,
but purrs her love. They give her heart a thrill.
Her kittens tumble near her, having fun.
A mother cat is dozing in the sun.

The Vulture

Behold the vulture.
He has no culture.
His dining habit
is road-kill rabbit.
If he comes looking
for my home-cooking
in hopes of munchin'
a sit-down luncheon
I'll have to slight him
and not invite him.

Billy's Revenge

A wild, lawyer's goat from South Tuttle,
accused by a geek, was not subtle,
but, intent on maiming,
hit where he was aiming
then calmly prepared for re-butt-al.

Heavenly Horses

Though often it is hard to reach the sky—
for we are prone to sin as I recall,
all horses go to heaven when they die.

Old Nell was such a gentle soul that I
devised a statue of her ten feet tall.
Though often it is hard to reach the sky,

her spirit dwells up there where angels fly.
She nibbles grain inside a golden stall.
All horses go to heaven when they die.

My Ned, with me astride his back, was spry.
His gentle gait would never let me fall.
Though often it is hard to reach the sky,

he dines on clover as soft breezes sigh
among enchanted hills where saints enthrall.
All horses go to heaven when they die.

I miss my kind companions. That is why
upon my heart their loss has cast a pall.
Though often it is hard to reach the sky,
all horses go to heaven when they die.

To A Pushy Cat

Tom,
I did not want you,
lop-eared interloper,
eight pound beggar.

Undaunted,
you clawed your way in,
demanded protection
from an uncaring world.

I fed you out of pity,
bathed you,
took care of your fleas.
It was the least I could do.

I could never need you,
not me, a cold hearted
resister of hypnotic purrs.
But you, my scruffy tailed
cuddles, my rainy day buddy,
have proven me wrong.
I am now your slave.

Hippo Choir

A three-headed hippo from Kenner
tap danced on the stage for his dinner.
He ended by swinging
his backside and singing
contralto, soprano and tenor.

The Abandoned Kittens

A mama cat has left her kittens here.
She must have known my heart is kind and true.
I love them all. One has a spotted ear.

Although her motives must have been sincere,
her vagrant attitude will never do.
A mama cat has left her kittens here.

I feed them from a bottle. It is clear
they need a mother's love to see them through.
I love them all. One has a spotted ear.

They scrabble in their box when night is near.
I pray that consolation will ensue.
A mama cat has left her kittens here.

Why did she run away? I truly fear
her babes' contented moments will be few.
I love them all. One has a spotted ear.

They frisk around my ankles and endear
themselves to me. I think they love me, too.
A mama cat has left her kittens here.
I love them all. One has a spotted ear.

Why The Charmed Snake Does Not Escape

A flute is played that charms the snake.
For cobra's sake
the music rings
of pleasant things.
The cobra watches as it sways,
devises ways
to disappear,
but it is clear
it will remain in basket there
upon the square,
for to the side
its tail is tied.

A Black Cat

Someday I want to be a black cat—
    just once.
I want to strut down the middle of the street,
make tires screech in superstition.
I want to see my teeth mirrored
    in a raven's eye.

I want to howl on the back fence
    for my lady love,
wriggle through spaces whisker wide
then purr my sleepy self into a daze.

I want to slink and creep.
I want to peek at ladies having tea
and disappear when they see me.

I want to doze in a garden
underneath tomato vines in summer,
not moving when dogs next door
    become incensed.
Someday I want to be a black cat—
    just once.

My Feathered Helpers—Where Did They Go?

I miss my red tailed hawk
that sits in the uppermost branch
of the sycamore tree.

I need him for my spirit's consolation.
He brings me peace, but not today.
Perhaps he skims the grain field
scaring up a mouse for breakfast.

Where are the turkey buzzards
that keep the roadway pristine
for my discriminating view?
Flattened skunk is on the menu.
There are no diners in sight.

All this summer various cacklers, caws,
and chirpers gleaned my garden
of aphids and other pests,
especially those horrid, black beetles
that now devour the squash
and the striped melon.

I must carry on without my feathered helpers.
I heard they went to Mexico
on a migratory wind.
It seems to me that birds have a way
of not being there when they are truly needed.

Missing

My little dog has run away.
If you should see him, please be kind.
I miss him more than I can say.
My little dog has run away.
I thought I saw him yesterday
sadly chewing a bacon rind.
My little dog has run away.
If you should see him, please be kind.

The Halloween Cat

On Halloween nobody knows
where Mr. Golden Whiskers goes.
His eyes of emerald green turn red.
He bounds across the garden bed,
jumps the fence and disappears
with eerie howls and laid back ears.
The north wind told me it believes
he guards the spirits of autumn leaves,
then guides the goblins as they pass
through doors and shuttered window glass.
I thought I saw him in the gloom
behind an old witch on her broom.
When his long journey is complete,
he wanders home on weary feet.
Then Mr. Golden Whiskers sighs
and looks around with haunted eyes.
He'll never tell the things he's seen.
He's had enough of Halloween.

Horned Toad Hangout

Horned toads adore a swarm of ants.
They eat them when they have a chance.
On any given day
they hurry to the smorgasbord
to dine upon the fiery horde
      at Lizard Land Café.

Ignoring vicious stings and bites,
the toads indulge their appetites
while victims rush around,
their only hope of living on,
a spot beneath a wedge of stone,
      or burrow in the ground.

At length, when sun is setting fast,
the connoisseurs depart at last,
replete with nature's fare.
They'll soon return to this same site
where they have found to their delight
      the plate is never bare.

Mockingbird

A mockingbird is singing on his throne.
His kingdom is a tree outside my door.
I often listen until night is gone
to every melody he keeps in store.
I wonder how such purity and grace
could be contained in one. Perhaps he flies
aloft to meet an angel face to face
who gives him music straight from paradise.
I only know old ghosts that creep and sigh
must leave when he begins his nightly tune.
Dark clouds must disappear and shadows fly
as he keeps watchful guard beneath the moon.

Sing, mocking bird, and keep my spirit strong.
You hold my heart together with your song.

A Rat's Reprieve

I heard commotion at my door.
My cat, Lenore,
had caught a rat.
That silly cat
seemed sure a present could not hurt.
A rat dessert
at lunch would be
a treat for me.
She gripped the poor thing in her jaws.
Its bloody paws
Were shaking so.
I said, "Let go!"
I pried it from her mouth. It shot
away and got
into a drain.
It squeaked in pain.
But, just before it disappeared,
all draggle-eared,
it looked at me with eyes aglow,
and even though
that rat was riled
I think it smiled.

haiku

guarding its nestlings
high on branch of red oak tree
jaybird dive bombs cat

She Won't Turn Loose Until It Thunders

I have acquired a lovely pet—
a turtle-ette
with scratching claws
and snapping jaws.
She bit my bosom buddy, Bruce.
She won't turn loose
till lightning zooms
and thunder booms.
It might be spring when she lets go,
a year of woe,
for lightning's out.
We're in a drought.

Cicadas Say

"Sheree, sheree," cicadas say,
monotonous to me, but they
most likely speak of children, grown
with young cicadas of their own,
or how the leaves are tasty green,
sautéed by summer's sultry sheen.

"Sheree, sheree," cicadas cry
their wildest tales of earth and sky,
repeat themselves from night till noon,
distract the stars and shake the moon.
Perhaps they wail of ice and snow,
of dreadful days when they must go.

"Sheree, sheree," cicadas sing.
Ecstatic on the wind, they bring
their finest music. Every tree
resounds in joyful melody.
I might rejoice and sing as well
if I knew half of what they tell.

haiku

       pine trees waft perfume
   downhill just before moonrise
      coyotes sniff the air

Canine Intellectual

A doggy sniffs his master's shoes,
and with his nose he reads the news.

Ladybug

My ladybug is on a stem.
She wears a dress of party red
with black dots ending at the hem.
My ladybug is on a stem.
She might go dancing on a whim
in Sister Johnson's flower bed.
My ladybug is on a stem.
She wears a dress of party red.

In Retrospect

I thought the owl was friend to me,
a cheerful fellow of the dark,
engaged to help my mind embark
on idle thoughts of reverie.

But that was when I was content
and you were here, my love, my light
to guard me safely through the night,
confirming what devotion meant.

You gave me promise of a day
that heaven would forever bless
and, in a state of happiness
I heard the owl cry far away.

Alone, I find I am not brave.
I wish the owl would hush and go.
I cannot bear his song of woe.
The sound is lonely as the grave.

Song Of Summer

Outside my door a cricket sings
a simple, summer lullaby
of woodland smoke and mountain springs.
Outside my door a cricket sings.
Above the south wind's murmurings
the cricket praises earth and sky.
Outside my door a cricket sings
a simple, summer lullaby.

At The Picnic

A bug is crawling down my neck
with clicking nails and spiky beard.
I must curtail its frenzied trek.
A bug is crawling down my neck.
I jump and shout. How could a speck
of protein make me feel so weird?
A bug is crawling down my neck
with clicking nails and spiky beard.

Bird Of Prey

At late evening a red-tailed hawk
eagerly scans the river. Alerted
by its shadow, the fish kingdom
hides. A startled frog leaps
     from a mossy stone.

The sun casts a final burst of light,
imbues the hawk with color
of fiery gold. It strikes. Sharp
talons spear an unwary snake.

High on a branch of a dead tree
it leisurely dines. Satisfied, unaware
of tomorrow's hunger, it sleeps as
it is swiftly consumed by insatiable night.

Robin

A robin is singing
a bright roundelay.
It ruffles its feathers
this dark winter day.

It hops down the fence rail
with notes of good cheer,
convincing me greatly
that springtime is here.

With snow on the roof top
and ice to the bone,
if it hadn't told me
I'd never have known.

Views

The Psychedelic Party

Today several of us colors
rode uptown on a lady's dress.
We enjoyed the trip until
she sat on Red and Yellow.
Then she spilled hot chocolate
on Green. He howled for hours.

We watched her try on hats.
None matched us. Her mouth
curled in a frustrated pout.
      Turquoise snickered.

Later at home she kicked us
onto the floor and clothed herself
in a purple summer frock.
      Into the washer we went.
Oops! She washed us in hot water.

We had quite a party. Everyone got drunk
      on laundry detergent.
We are paying for it now—all of us
one shade—murky pink.

Age, The Cat

Age is the feline of my days.
Boldly she stalks me
    with hisses and growls.

Once, she was merely a kitten,
batting at my youth with playful
paws. That was before I grew whiskers
    and coarse, gray hair.

She's serious now.
Tail twitching, she watches
    my every move,
forces me down mazes of despair
    until I, cringing, hide
in a corner, waiting for the bite
    of her powerful jaws.

Barbie

For years I tried to emulate her style,
became a blonde. My legs grew long and thin.
I later married someone known as Ken,
who fell in love with my attractive smile.
The fairy tale was lovely for a while
until I realized I could not win.
Barbie is perfect, not like I have been.
I had to back away lest I defile

her image, for my face is flawed from life.
I bear the bitter scars of time while she
resides inside her box, aloof and sure

of painless days, immune to any strife.
I crave her plastic immortality,
for I am of the earth and must endure.

Little Boy Love—For Tony

Little boy smiles are coupons
to be used on a rainy day
when I am sad and he is grown
and lives too far away.

Little boy dreams are treasures
to be garnered one by one
like pearls from the deepest ocean,
or gold from the brightest sun.

Little boy hugs are roses
whose many hues impart
a velvet love forever
on the trellis of my heart.

Death Of A Vacuum Cleaner

Promoters of efficient bristles,
      contented hums, makers of those
      sleek machines that live in our closets,
never witness the death throes of one
that has been gagged on dog hair
for twenty years, or bludgeoned by
      sharp corners, ruptured by pennies
      and nails until it screams like a maniac
trying to prove it can still gobble dirt with gusto.

Lights flashing, it becomes a derelict,
      wobbles across the floor, begs mercy
      from a frustrated owner.
Perhaps a final sweep around the room
can be coaxed from it before it strips its gears.
When it dies, its innards must be inspected
      for what went wrong.
      I lost mine today, gave it a screwdriver
autopsy, an oil can eulogy, a junk heap burial.
      I shall mourn its death forever.

In This Land

Had freedom never been reality
for me, I might be happy as a slave,
in love with every shackle binding me,
an innocent, from childhood to the grave.

Sustained by love and liberty, I share
endeavors for a better life. My goal
is never to succumb to hatred's snare,
or wear the tarnish of a traitor's soul.

In foreign lands where tyranny is king,
dictators wield their swords and never sleep.
Imprisoned subjects there can only sing
their broken songs of misery. I weep

because their chains will never let them fly,
for I am blessed with wings that touch the sky.

The Missing Poet

I wonder where that poet went
whose verse could make me laugh and cry.
Her writing is a sacrament.
I wonder where that poet went.
I wish she would return in print.
She disappeared without goodbye.
I wonder where that poet went
whose verse could make me laugh and cry.

To Keep My Leaping Sheep

My herd of woolies must have run away.
I searched for them, but only ten remain.
At night I count them one by one and pray
they do not disappear, for it is plain
I need them for insomnia's despair.
They give me courage, as I lie awake,
bring comfort as they hurtle through the air
of my imagination. For my sake
they hypnotize me into dreams awhile
until the morning sunlight. Never slow,
intelligent and faithful, blessed with style
they never fail to soothe me. Lately though,

that I not overtire them—precious sheep,
I jump the fence myself and let them sleep.

At Daybreak

If they ask you where I am, love,
please tell them I have gone
north with a cold wind wandering
 over a land alone
where tomorrow never ends—
 the days are made of stone.

They'll come to our door one morning
when leaves are brown and sere.
Perhaps they will find you weeping
 because I am not here.
Just tell them I am settled in
 the blue of my own star
where my soul has quite forgotten
what earth and people are.

The Ticking Of The Clock

The old black clock has ticked my life away.
At twenty-one I laughed and watched it go.
At eighty-five I hope for one more day.

The hands move on. I cannot make them stay,
as ever more elusive moments flow.
The old black clock has ticked my life away.

The ghosts of all my years arrive and play
across its face. Their dance I do not know.
At eighty-five I hope for one more day.

When I was young my thoughts would often stray
to later years, for time was moving slow.
The old black clock has ticked my life away.

It hangs upon the wall and will not say
how long I have until the trumpets blow.
At eighty-five I hope for one more day.

As now I live in age, I often pray
the clock stands still. Its minutes are my foe.
The old black clock has ticked my life away.
At eighty-five I hope for one more day.

Behold The Raging River

The old Red River rages on its way
in waves—uncounted miles of mud and sand.
It was a timid stream just yesterday
before the rains arrived and took command.

In waves—uncounted miles of mud and sand,
it surges to the Gulf of Mexico.
Before the rains arrived and took command,
the river was a gentle lamb, and slow.

It surges to the Gulf of Mexico
from Palo Duro, its beginning place.
The river was a gentle lamb, and slow
with skies of April mirrored on its face.

From Palo Duro, its beginning place,
it gains momentum, whirling on and on
with skies of April mirrored on its face,
now cold and dark, with beauty, dead and gone.

It gains momentum, whirling on and on,
a demon none can tame forever more.
Now cold and dark, with beauty, dead and gone,
it plunges on, to reach a peaceful shore.

A demon none can tame forever more,
it was a timid stream just yesterday.
It plunges on, to reach a peaceful shore.
The old Red River rages on its way.

The Winner

When blows of earth have done their work on me,
and I am stunned too blind to see the sun—
When all becomes a maze I can't resolve,
I'll joy to know I lived for love and won.

They'll put me on a funeral bed of silk
to mourn the scars love gave me in my quest
while deeper wounds of life remain unseen,
engraved in rage by those I loved the best.

Too sad for tears, my friends at end of day
may look through twilight sky and see me run
exultantly, toward eternity,
a fool who lived for love and barely won.

Completing My Unfinished Poems

At times, unfinished sonnets hide in trees.
Quatrains escape and sail across the sky.
Sestinas disappear on sudden sprees.
My crippled villanelles sneak off and die.
My inability becomes a curse.
I cannot conjure visions, or compose.
An empty page is like a universe
without its stars when inspiration goes.
But it returns, rekindles old desire
to reach elusive treasures from the past.
They gather at the window, seeking fire
I hold within forever. Moving fast,

I grab my long abandoned pen and write.
The Muse is bringing lovely gifts tonight.

The New Year's Kiss

If I kissed him, my darling,
on New Year's Eve,
it's not what your eyes
would have you believe.

I kissed him for laughter.
I kissed him for tears.
I kissed him for pain
and long, passing years.

I know that your jealous heart
never forgives,
but the reason I kissed him
is because he lives.

When Love Dies

When love dies, there is a moan,
a sound like winter coming on
with two souls reaching out of place
to satisfy one last embrace.

When love dies, there is a cry
unheard by strangers passing by,
but hidden in a land apart.
The dreadful screaming of the heart
goes on and on until it spills
and dies among life's lonely hills.

When love dies, there is a wail
that none who play at love foretell
before old sorrow calls its own
to stumble through the dark alone,
unresurrected by healing years,
pleas of regret, or solemn tears.

Listening To The Police Band Radio

Those nightly crimes fill me with dread.
There's always something going on.
Sometimes there is exchange of lead.
Those nightly crimes fill me with dread.
Why aren't those people home in bed
instead of causing siren's drone?
Those nightly crimes fill me with dread.
There's always something going on.

Toward Our Destinies

We are all like rivers
struggling toward a sea of freedom,
avoiding dams of destruction,
forcing ourselves around
boulders of disillusionment,

flowing on, forever hoping
not to end our days in
brackish back waters of despair,
stagnant and alone—with the crocodiles.

Dance, Gypsy

Dance, Gypsy, dance
with firelight in your eyes.
Dance for the golden fields.
Dance on the rim of sorrow.
Whirl, Gypsy, whirl
on moon-maddened feet.
Lose your daily care
for wandering's tomorrow.

Turn, Gypsy, turn,
as does the whole earth turning.
Spin for your sip of life
from silver goblets flowing.
Dance, Gypsy, dance,
wild with your song of living,
leaving the elements trembling
goodbye at your caravan's going.

At Parting

The time has come and now we say adieu.
Our lives diverge and we must be apart,
but friendship is a star, forever true,
as long as it resides within the heart.
Our star has led us to this final day—
a day of much regret. Our words, sincere,
we speak of fate and what it takes away
before we reminisce and shed a tear.

I shall remember days of long ago
when kindred souls made happy moments fly.
We treasure what we have, and now I know
that I shall miss you as the years go by,

for we have been a long, long way, my friend.
I hope to meet you at the journey's end.

October Memories

It seems so long ago that you and I
explored October's byways hand in hand,
aflame with love we thought would never die,
but we were young and did not understand
the ruse of time—how it would slip away
in shadows, causing us to part. Alone,
I find our romance was inclined to stay
no longer than a rose whose bloom has flown.
It rains across the hills. The cold is deep.
Where are those golden dreams that used to be?
No sun filled hours shall warm me as I sleep.
Bare winter nights obscure all memory,

but, when October skies are hazy blue,
I wander country lanes and think of you.

Competitive Brawl

In yearly competition sonnets vie
with villanelles and other forms, for place.
Sestina soldiers raise their weapons high,
obliterate quatrains and soon erase
those rabid roundelays, but then the brawl
may shift itself and lurch the other way.
The horns of war will sound as verses fall
to up-start limericks that join the fray.
Impatient judges must be calm and wait
for victors to emerge in grace and style.
Uncertainty will slowly dissipate.
The battle will be over in a while.

The end results make happy poets grin
when trampled words revise, arise and win.

Grandpa's Outfit

When Grandpa passed away, we heard
the undertaker cry,
"Where are his Gucchi shoes and socks?
His silken shirt, his tie?"

"Our dear departed souls must wear
the very best. I fear
if you don't bring him proper garb,
you'll never park him here."

We had a fight, an awful fight,
but we prevailed, and fast.
Our grandpa lies in peaceful sleep,
a pilgrim, home at last.

His vest, canary yellow and
his pants, unholy red,
I hope he makes a stir among
the prim and proper dead.

Shadows

My friend,
I pray for you,
lost in dementia's land.
No one can understand
your world, askew.
Life's end

should be,
not blurry gray,
but bright with morning sun
where skies and clouds have spun
a perfect day.
I see

you've gone
beyond the light,
yet, God, in perfect grace,
will never let you face
eternal night
alone.

Exhibition

Graffiti on the morning train
might bring disdain.
Those rainbow lines
in bold designs
are not for everyone who waits
at crossing gates.
But I have found
scenes that astound,
am pleased that from the continent
artists have sent
a gallery
to dazzle me.

Immortal Love

Love never dies. Its many traces
hide in the shadows here and there.
It waits in old, forgotten places
to catch a stranger unaware.

Day Dreams

My Siamese and I have run away
in dreams, to Egypt where the sand is white.
She purrs a gentle tune this winter day.

As harem girl with colored scarves, I sway
with burnished dancers weaving left and right.
My Siamese and I have run away.

When we grow tired of desert airs, we may
escape to Cairo when the moon is bright.
She purrs a gentle tune this winter day.

Her azure eyes, half open, seem to say:
Conjure a handsome prince in blazing light!
My Siamese and I have run away.

The sleet is on the windowpane. I pray
We do not waken to that dreary sight.
She purrs a gentle tune this winter day.

Until the storm is past we must obey
that camel song that lures us with its might.
My Siamese and I have run away.
She purrs a gentle tune this winter day.

In My Hammock

It's a doodlebug day,
blue Popsicle sky.
White clouds drift away
and so do I.

Calico mama cat
lies drowsing in shade.
Summer's an old straw hat
and pink lemonade.

City bees droning past,
drunk on primrose wine,
lull me to sleep at last.
Summer's divine.

The Charms Of Spring

Spring ventured into town today
upon an April breeze.
She called the bluebirds out to play
and woke the honey bees.

She caused the morning sun to spill
its warmth from golden skies.
She sprinkled clover on the hill
complete with butterflies.

She snapped her fingers and white crowds
of daisies came her way.
She smiled and blessed the sky with clouds
she'd saved for such a day.

And way down in the meadow where
the weeping willow grows
she shook the sparkles from her hair
and blushed into a rose.

His Presence, Everywhere

Who has seen the hands of God?
In truth I say, not I,
but I have seen the red and gold
He painted on the sky.

Who has heard the voice of God?
I surely do not know,
but I have heard a gentle song
when evening breezes blow.

Who has seen the eyes of God?
Not many, it appears,
but I have seen the thunderclouds
grow heavy with His tears.

Who has read the mind of God?
No one, and yet He rings
His thoughts across the universe
and all creation sings.

Who has known the love of God?
I truly cannot say,
but, when I feel it in my heart,
it takes my breath away.

At Twilight

Although I pray with all my might,
the sunlight will not stay.
It drifts into the western dark,
disperses ray by ray.
I wish that I could keep it here
for never ending day,
to furnish solace for my soul
and chase the ghosts away.

In Tribute

When I was born, my mother, in her quest
for nurture, brought me comfort night and day,
endured the worst that I might have the best,
was swift to guide when I had lost my way.

When I was sad, I always found her there.
She wiped my tears and cheered me with a song.
She raised me with devotion and a prayer
that I might grow in wisdom and be strong.

Reluctantly, she vanished into night,
but memories sustain me even now.
Because she truly cared, my life is bright
without regret for yesteryear. Somehow

in increments that set my soul aglow,
I feel the love she gave me long ago.

Greener Grass

He asked her for a date,
but hope became despair,
for she said, "No, I cannot go.
I have to wash my hair."

He brought a single rose
and knocked upon her door.
By her disdain she made it plain
she thought he was a bore.

He begged on bended knee
for her to be his wife,
but she was keen to treat him mean.
She said, "Not on your life!"

She saw him yesterday.
Her sneer became a frown.
On his arm, was his latest charm—
that blonde who models uptown.

About The Author

LaVern Spencer McCarthy began writing poetry at age ten. She won first place and one dollar for a poem she entered in her elementary school class contest, and was hooked on writing and entering poetry contests thereafter.

She is the author of <u>Letters From My Heart</u> and <u>Dream Shadows,</u> a book co-authored with her son, Anthony Dickson, and <u>My Parrot Loves Me,</u> a book of humorous verse.

Her poetry has been published in *Cappers Weekly, Home Life Magazine, A Texas Garden of Verses,* National Federation of State Poetry Society's *Encore,* Poetry Society of Texas *A Book of The Year,* and *A Galaxy of Verse*, as well as numerous state anthologies and newspaper columns.

She is a member of Poetry Society of Texas, Poetry Society of Oklahoma, Austin Poetry Society, Poets Roundtable of Arkansas, and League of Minnesota Poets.

She has won over five hundred state awards and eighteen national awards for her poetry. LaVern lives in Blair, Oklahoma, with her son, a dachshund, and several spoiled cats.

Publishing History

Several of these poems have been published before.

A Galaxy of Verse—National Anthology
Poets At Work—Pennsylvania
Pennsylvania Poetry Society—Prize Poems
Austin Poetry Society—*Best Austin Poets*
Ohio Poetry Day—*Best of Ohio Contest Awards,*
Mississippi Poetry Society—*MPS Poetry Journal*
Pennsylvania Poetry Society Newsletter

Made in the USA
Monee, IL
04 January 2023